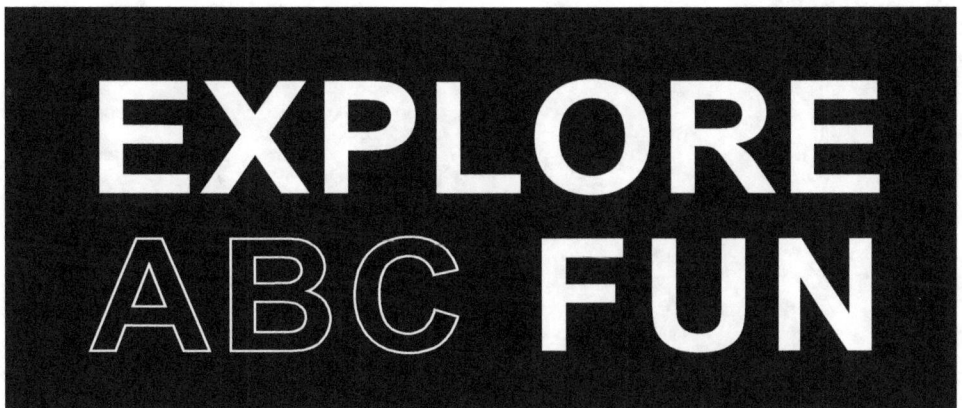

EXPLORE ABC FUN
COLORING BOOK

An Assembled Alphabet Adventure

written and illustrated by

CATHY ROWE

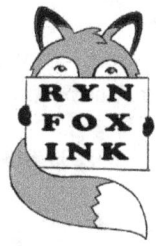

RYN
FOX
INK

Exploring ABC Fun Coloring Book
Written and Illustrated by Cathy Rowe© 2018

Printed in the United States of America

Cover design and book layout by
Claire Flint Last at Luminare Press
www.LuminarePress.com

Ryn Fox Ink
923 Hazelwood Dr.
Oregon City, OR 97045
www.RynFoxInk.com

ISBN: 978-0-9997513-2-9

For V

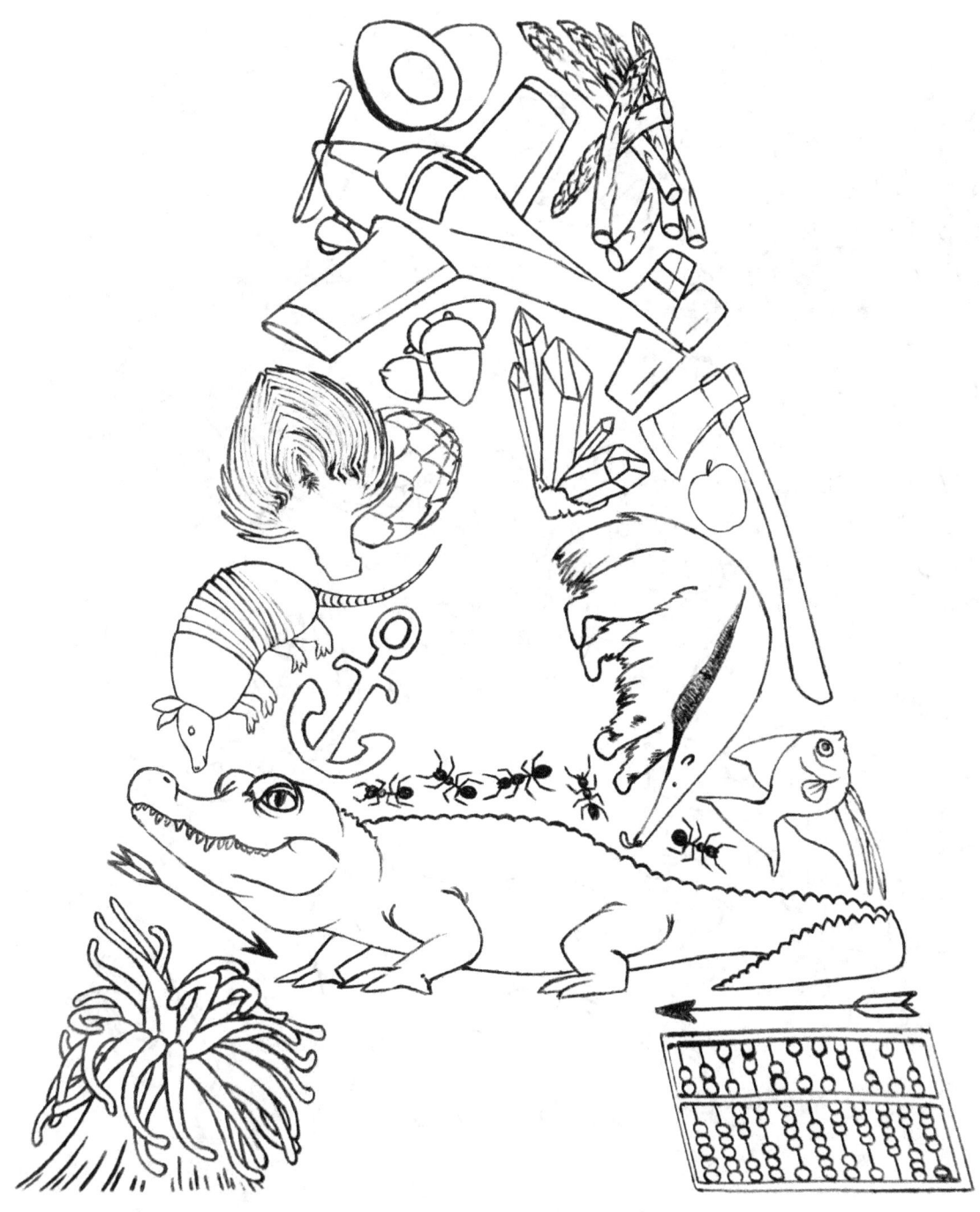

Can you find these objects?

Abacus, Acorns, Airplane, Alligator, Amethyst, Anchor, Anemone, Angelfish, Ant, Anteater, Apple, Armadillo, Arrow, Artichoke, Asparagus, Avocado, Axe

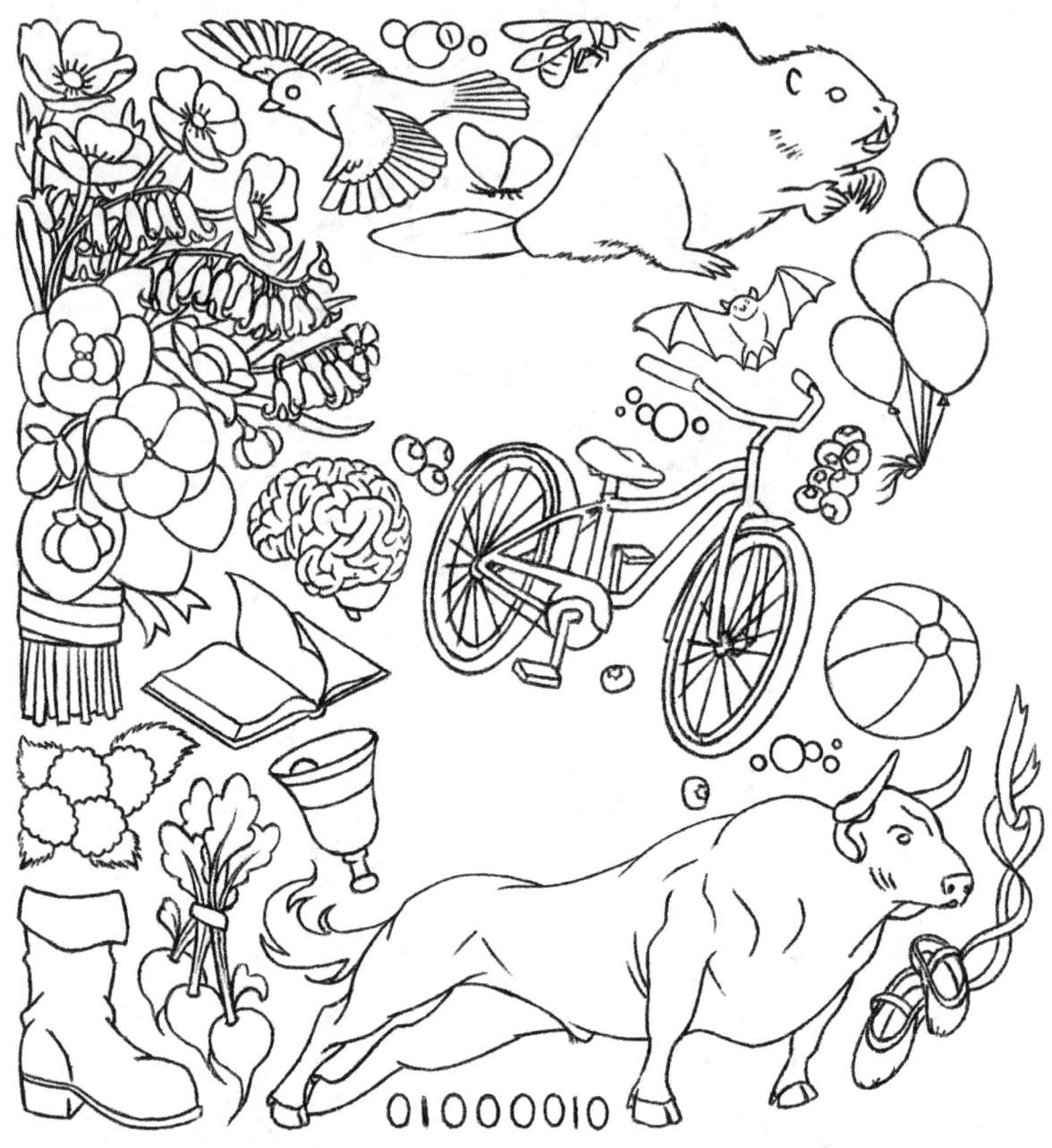

01000010

Look for these things.

Ballet Slippers, Balloons, Bat, Beach Ball, Beaver, Beets, Bell, Bicycle, Begonias, Binary Code, Blackberries, Blueberries, Bluebells, Bluebird, Book, Boot, Bouquet of Blossoms, Brain, Bubbles, Bull, Bumblebee, Buttercups, Butterfly

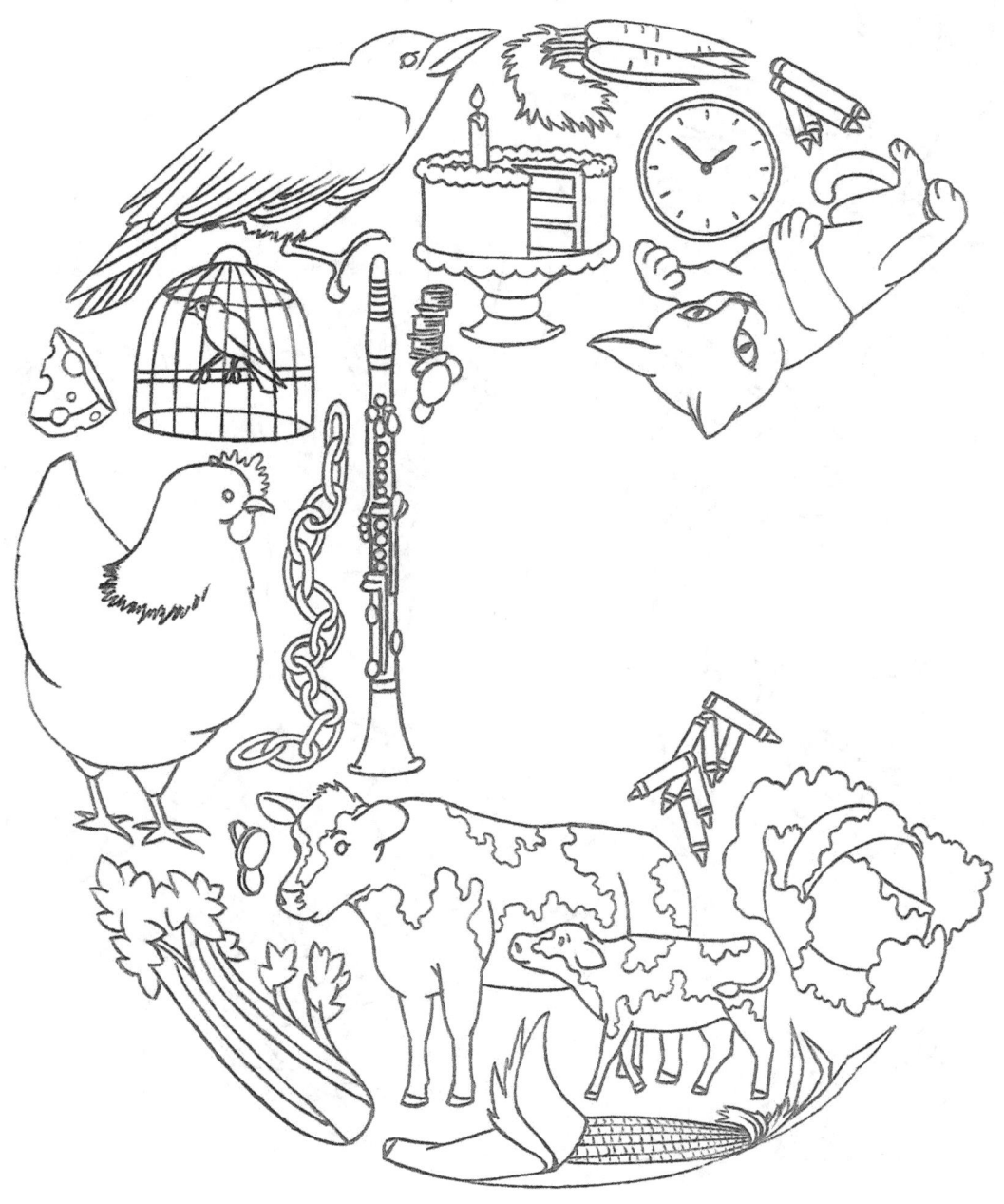

Do you see...

Cabbage, Caged Canary, Cake, Candle, Cat, Celery, Chain, Cheese, Chicken, Clarinet, Clock, Coins, Corn, Cow, Crayons, Crow

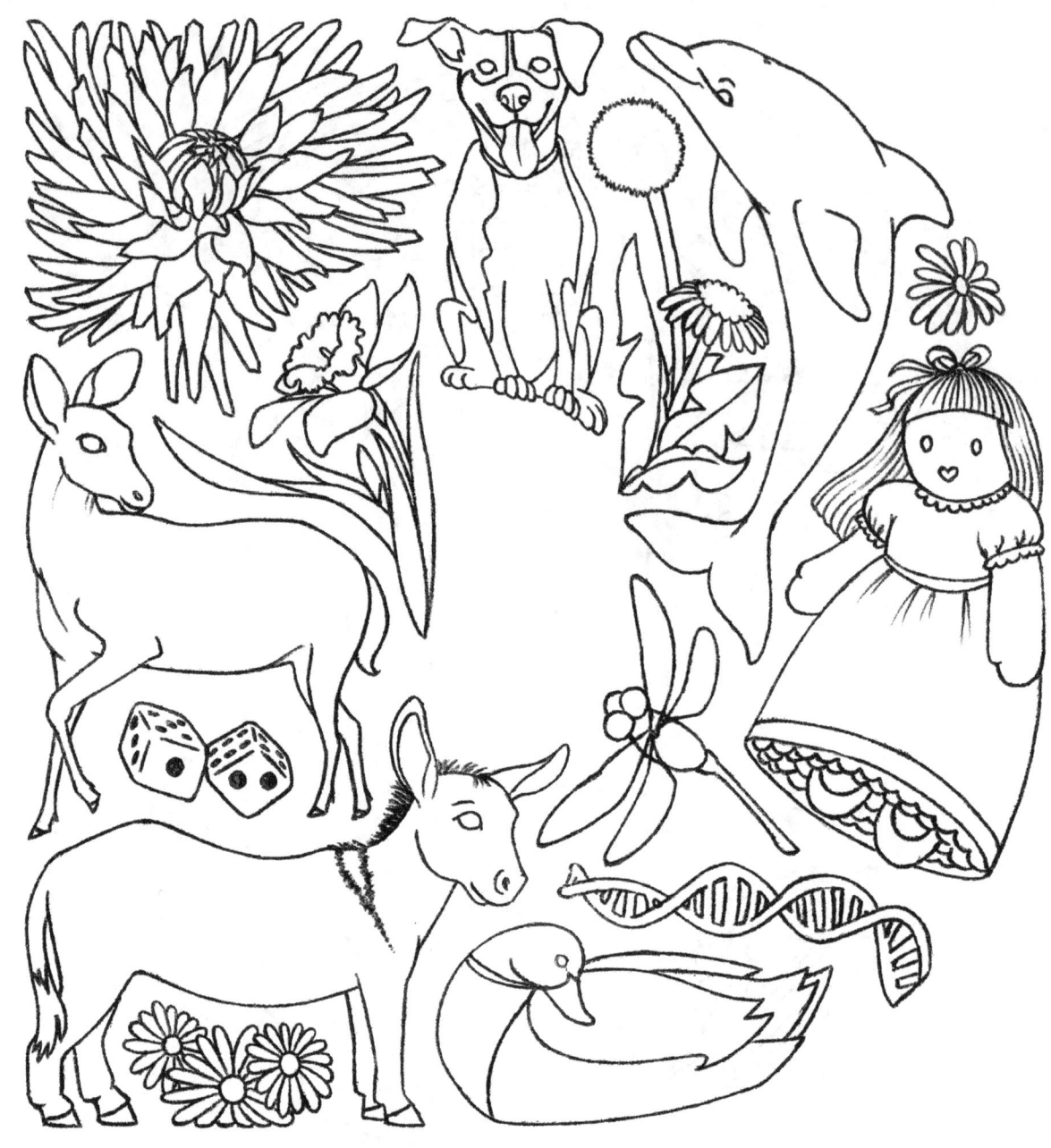

Look for these objects.

Dahlia, Daisy, Dandelion, Daffodil, Deer, Dice, DNA, Dog, Doll, Dolphin, Donkey, Dragonfly, Duck

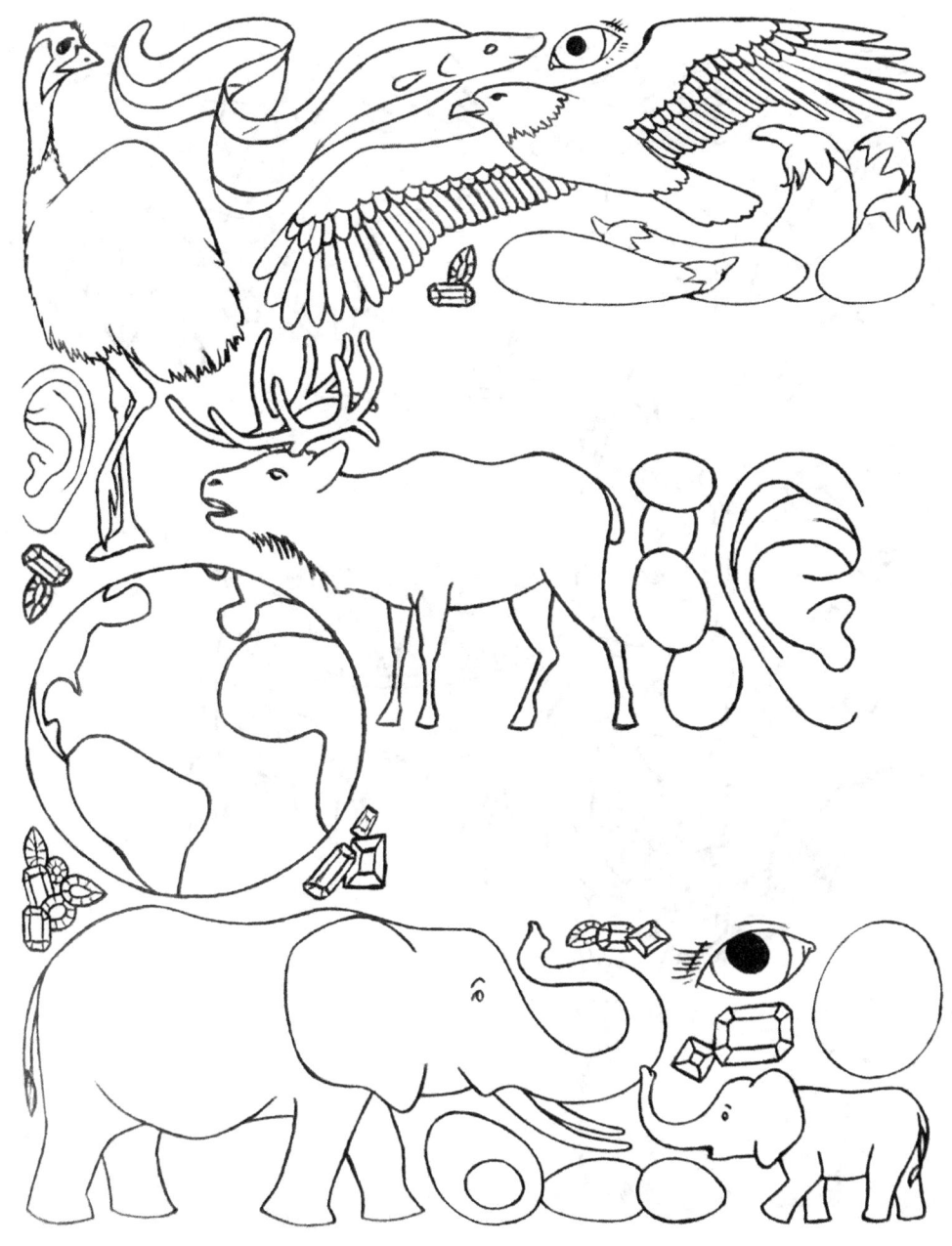

Do you see these things?

Eagle, Ear, Earth, Eel, Egg, Eggplant, Elephant, Elk, Emerald, Emu, Eye

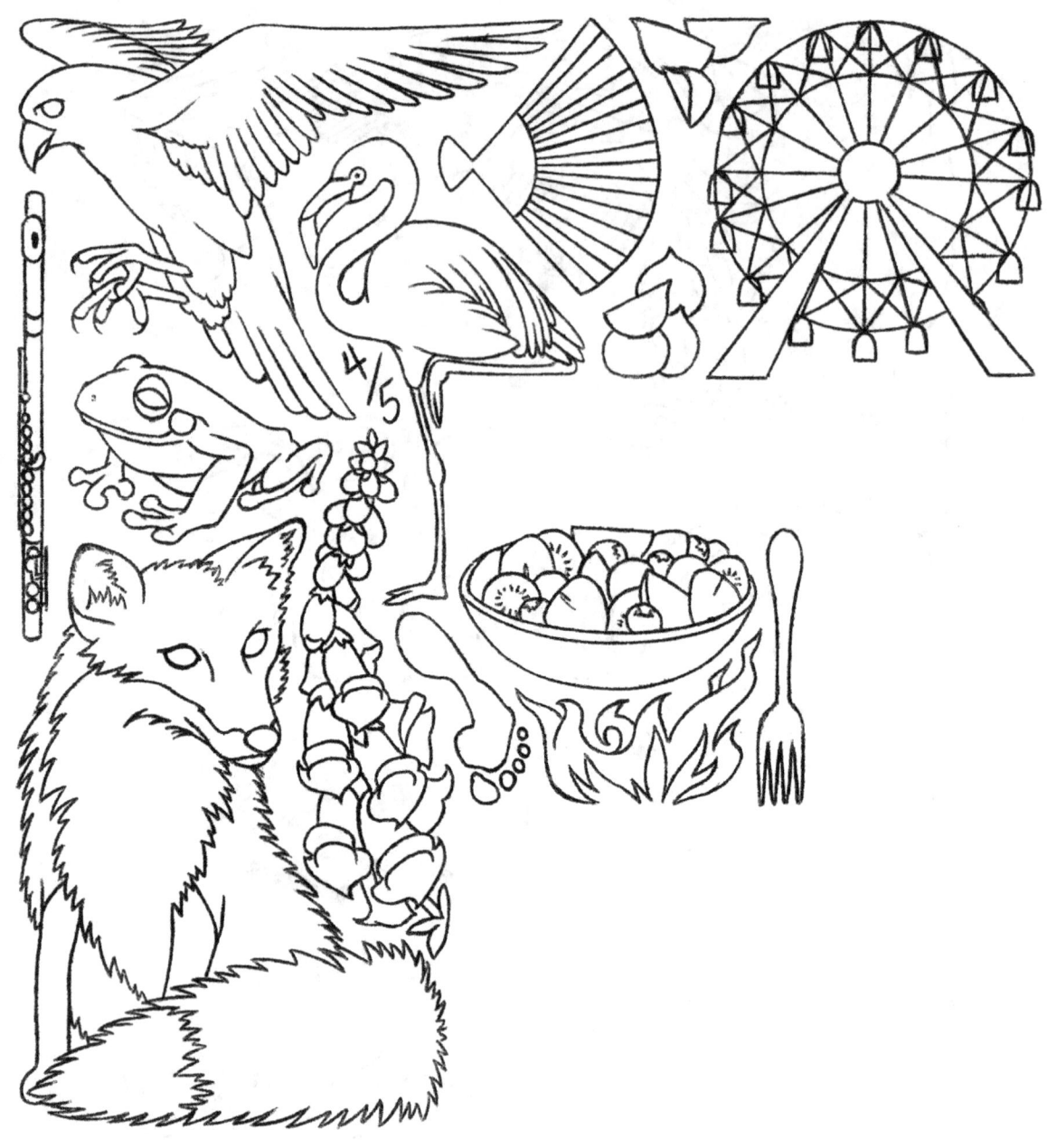

Can you find...

Falcon, Fan, Ferris Wheel, Fig, Fire, Flamingo, Flute, Footprint, Fork, Four Fifths Fraction, Fox, Foxgloves, Frog, Fruit Salad

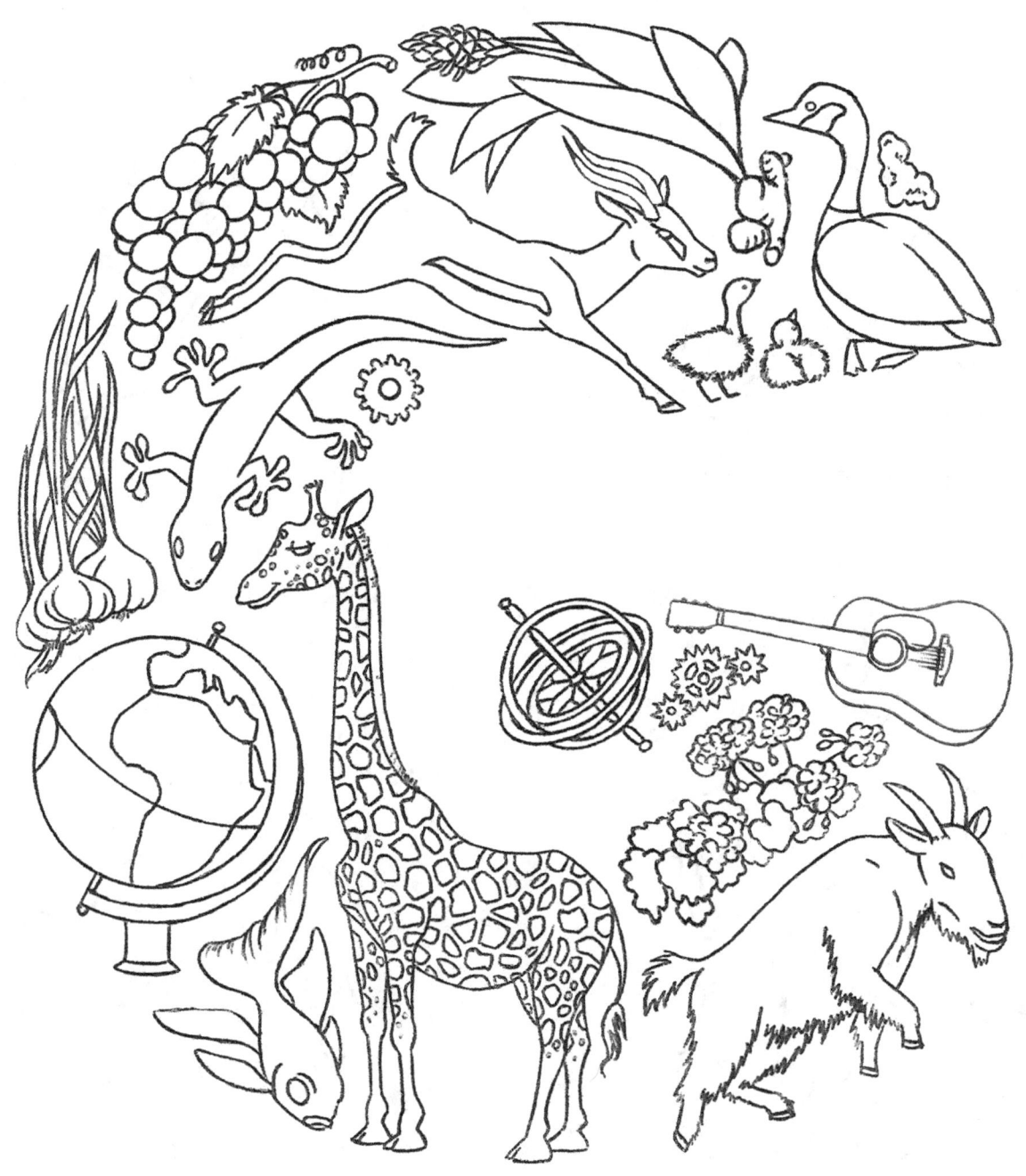

Do you see these objects?

Garlic, Gazelle, Gears, Gecko, Geranium, Ginger, Giraffe, Globe, Goat, Gold, Goldfish, Goose, Gosling, Grapes, Guitar, Gyroscope

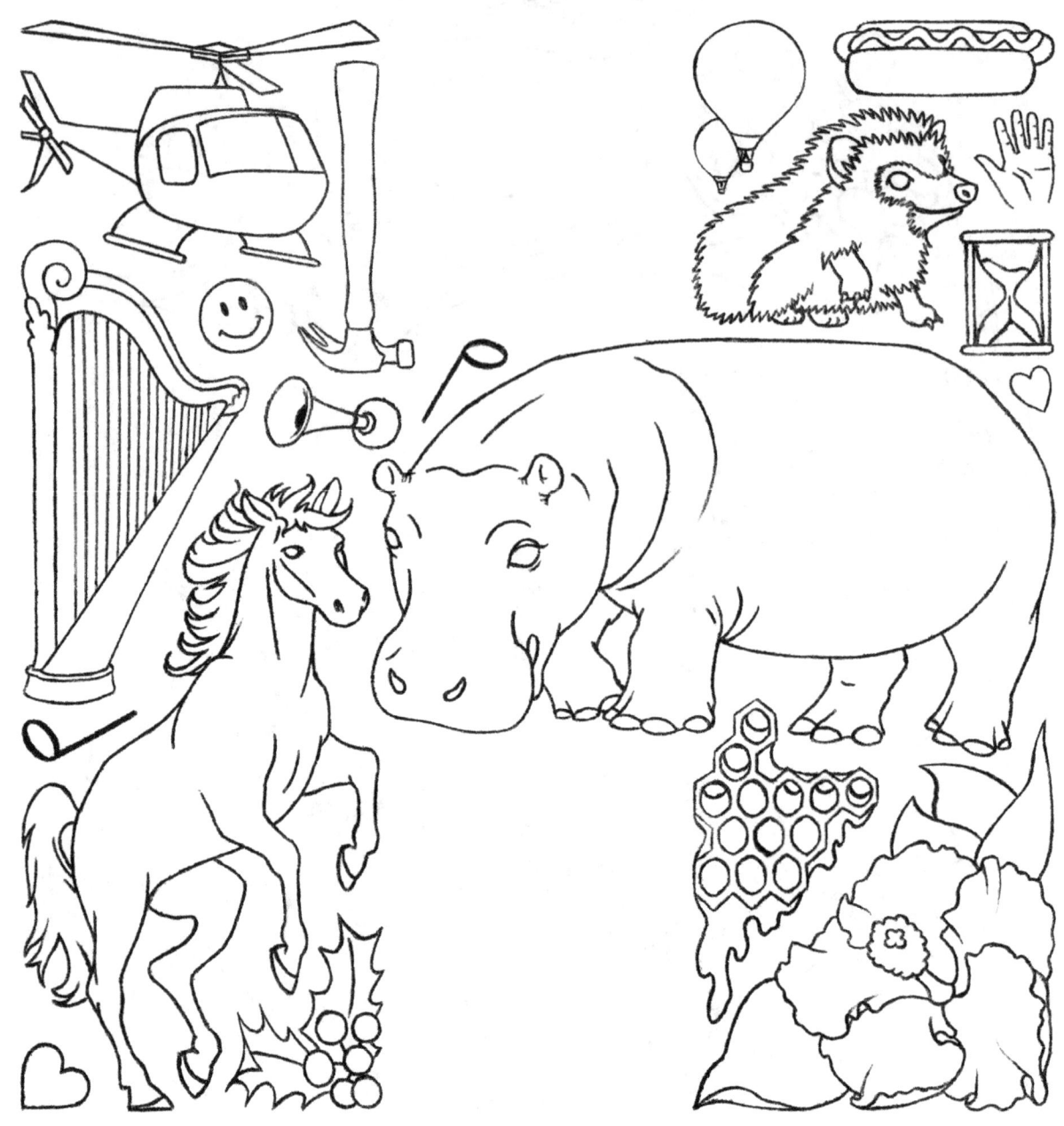

Can you find these things?

Half Note, Hammer, Happy Face, Harp, Heart, Hedgehog, Helicopter, Hibiscus, Hippopotamus, Holly, Honeycomb, Horn, Horse, Hotdog, Hot-Air Balloon, Hourglass

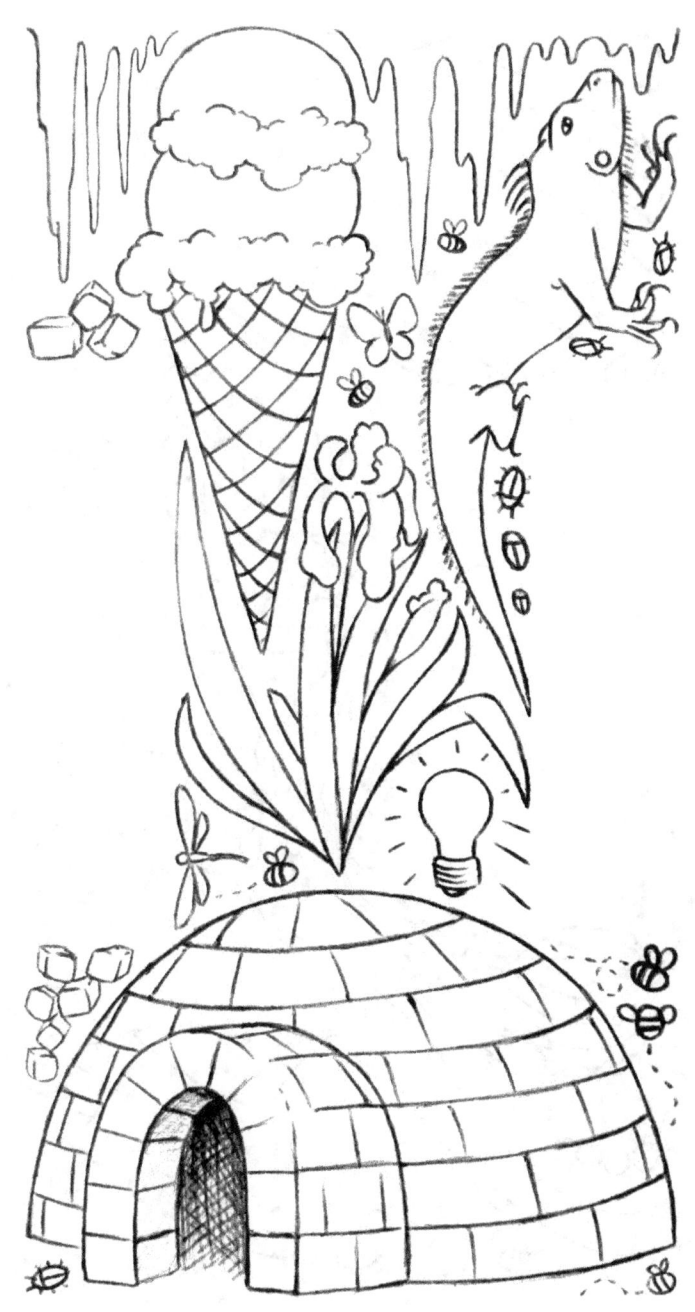

Look for...

Ice Cream, Ice Cubes, Icicles, Idea, Igloo, Iguana, Insects, Iris

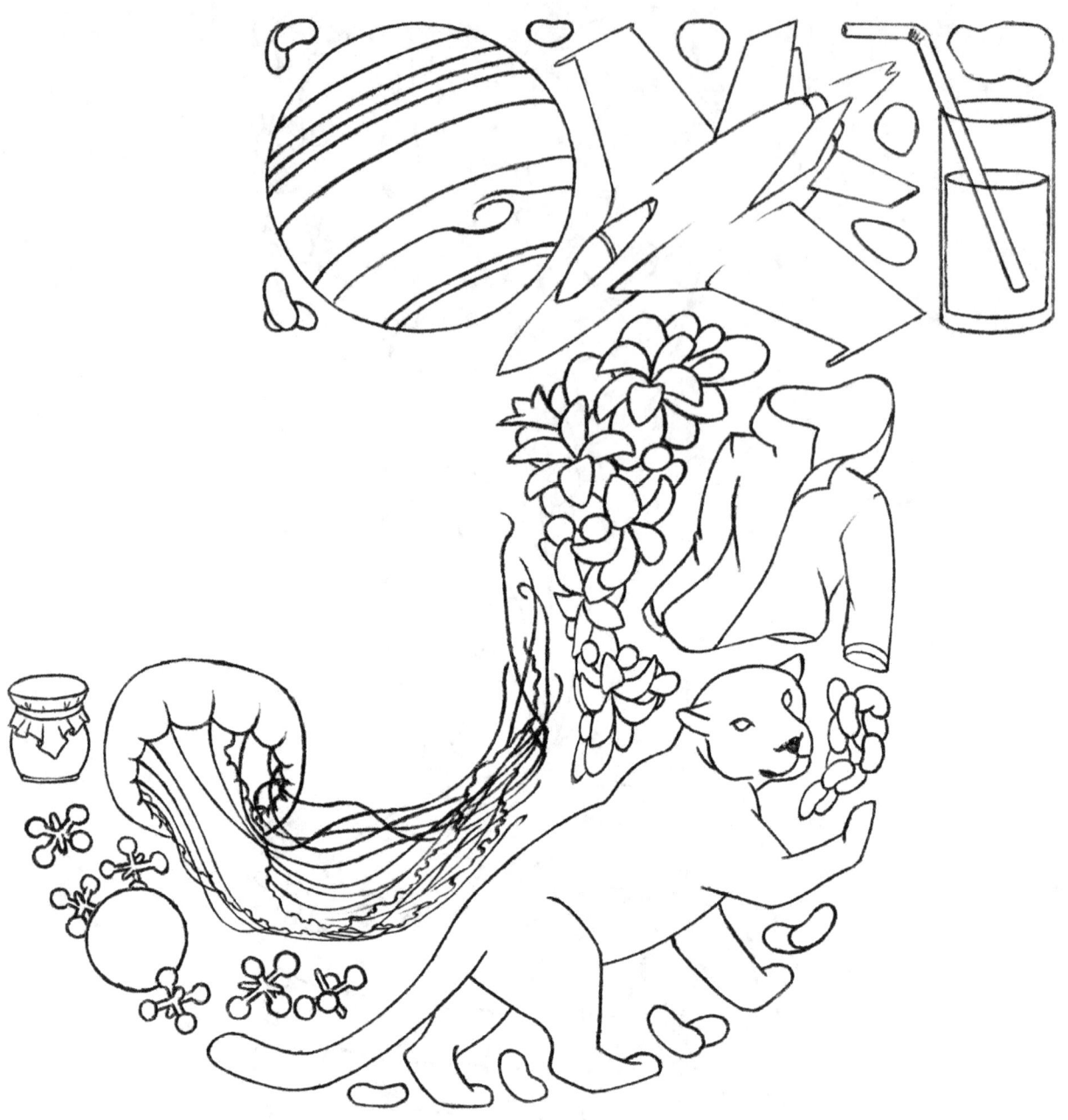

Can you find these objects?

Jacks, Jade, Jacket, Jaguar, Jar of Jam, Jasmine, Jasper, Jellyfish, Jellybeans, Jet, Juice, Jupiter

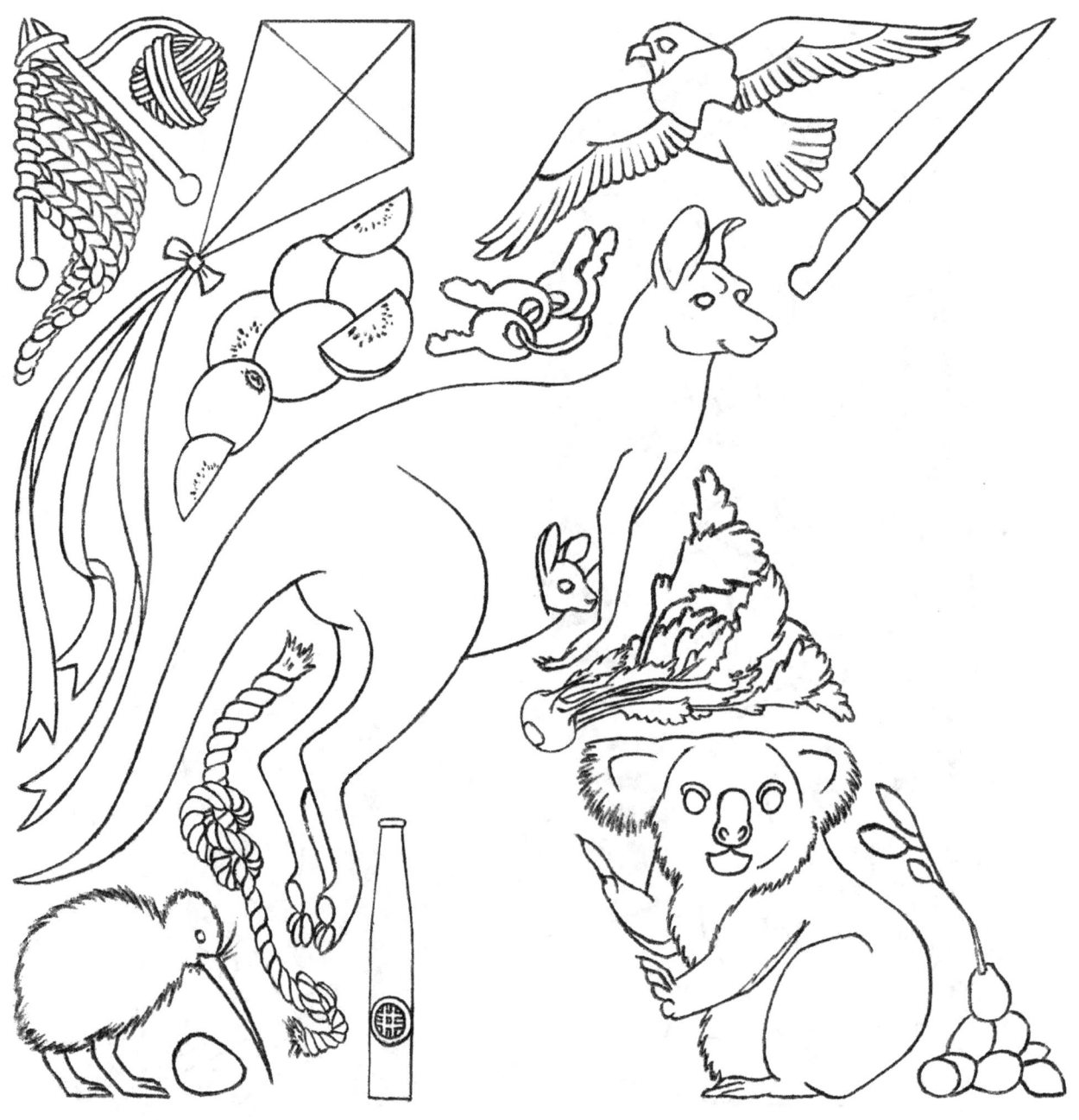

Look for these things.

Kangaroo, Kazoo, Keys, Kestrel, Kite, Kiwi Bird, Kiwi Fruit, Knife, Knitting, Knot, Koala, Kohlrabi, Kumquat

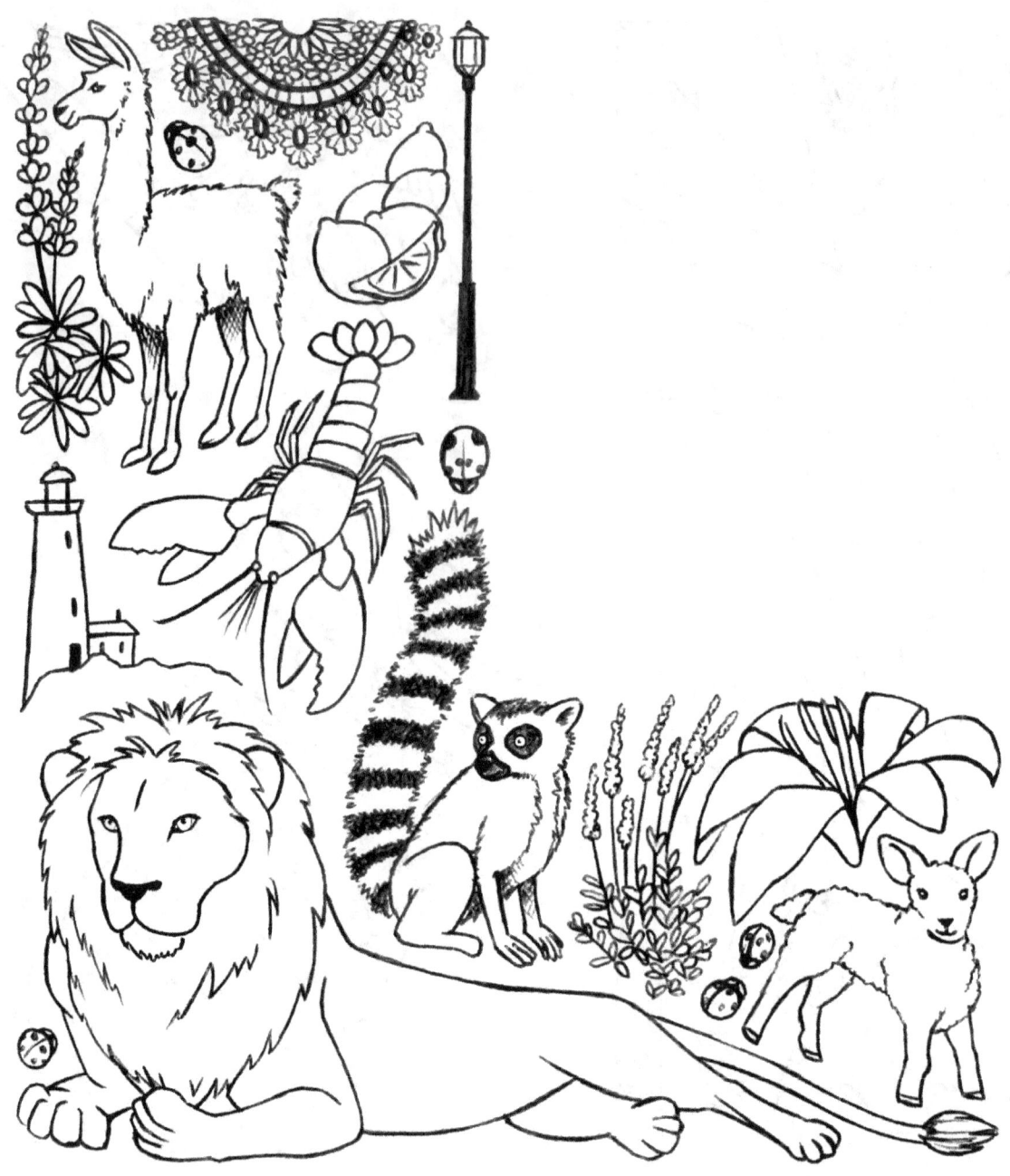

Do you see...

Lace, Ladybug, Lamb, Lamppost, Lavender, Lemons and Limes, Lemur, Lighthouse, Lily, Lion, Llama, Lobster, Lupin

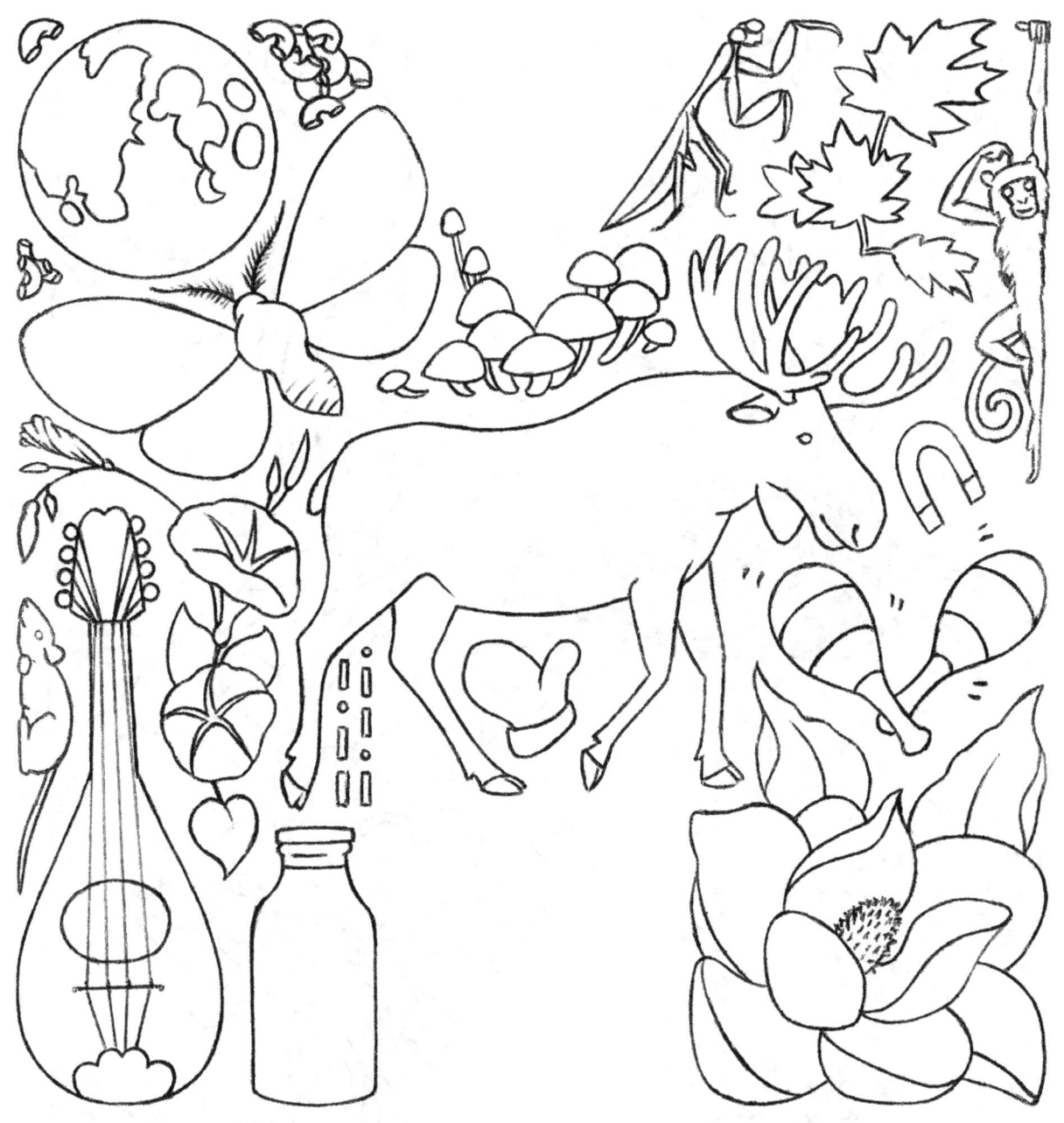

Look for these objects.

Macaroni, Magnet, Magnolia, Mandolin, Mantis, Maple Leaf, Maracas, Milk, Mitten, Monkey, Moon, Moose, Mouse, Morning Glory, Morse Code, Moth, Mushrooms

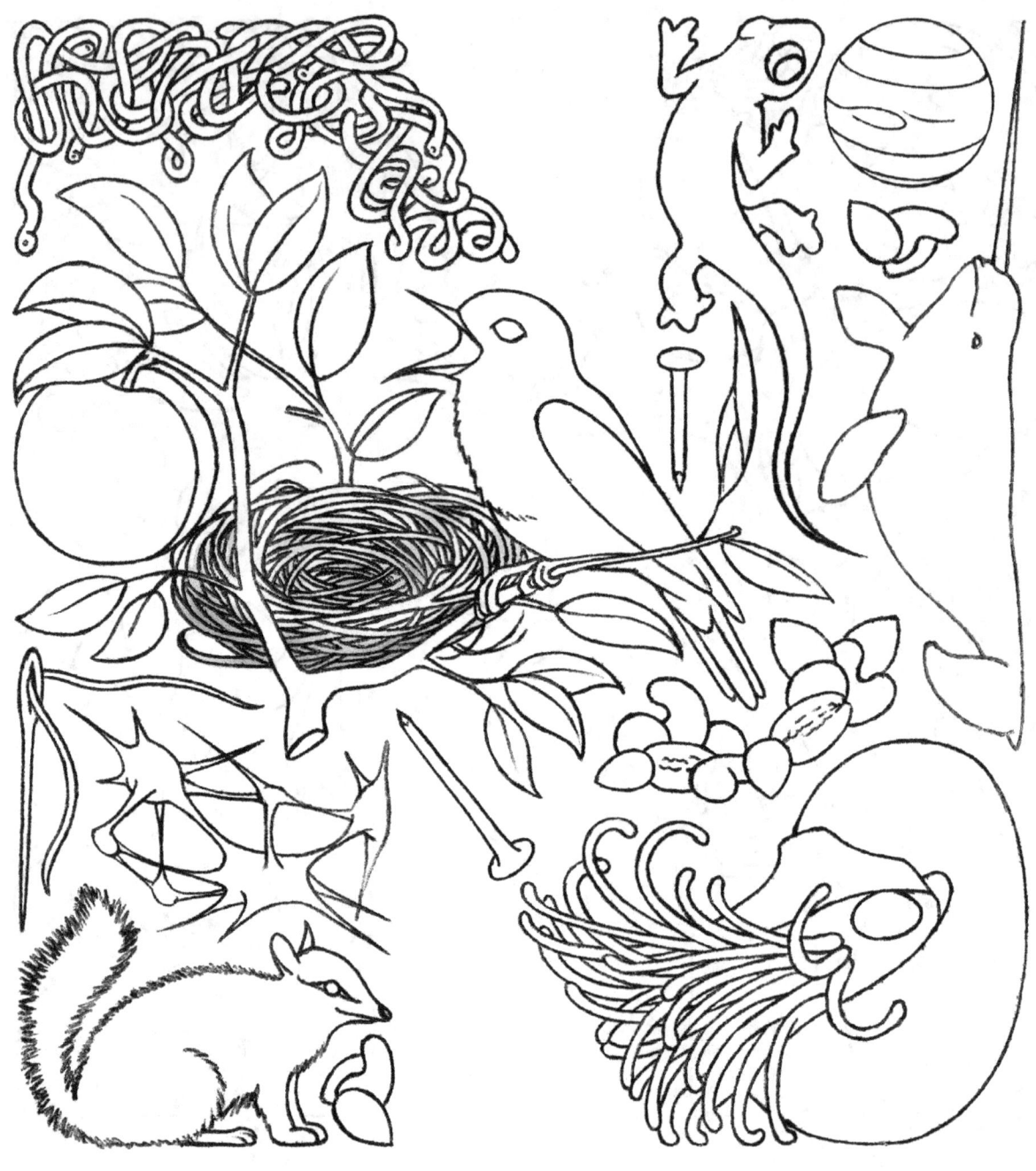

Do you see these things?

Nail, Narwhal, Nautilus, Nectarine, Needle, Neptune, Nest, Neuron, Newt, Nightingale, Noodles, Numbat, Nuts

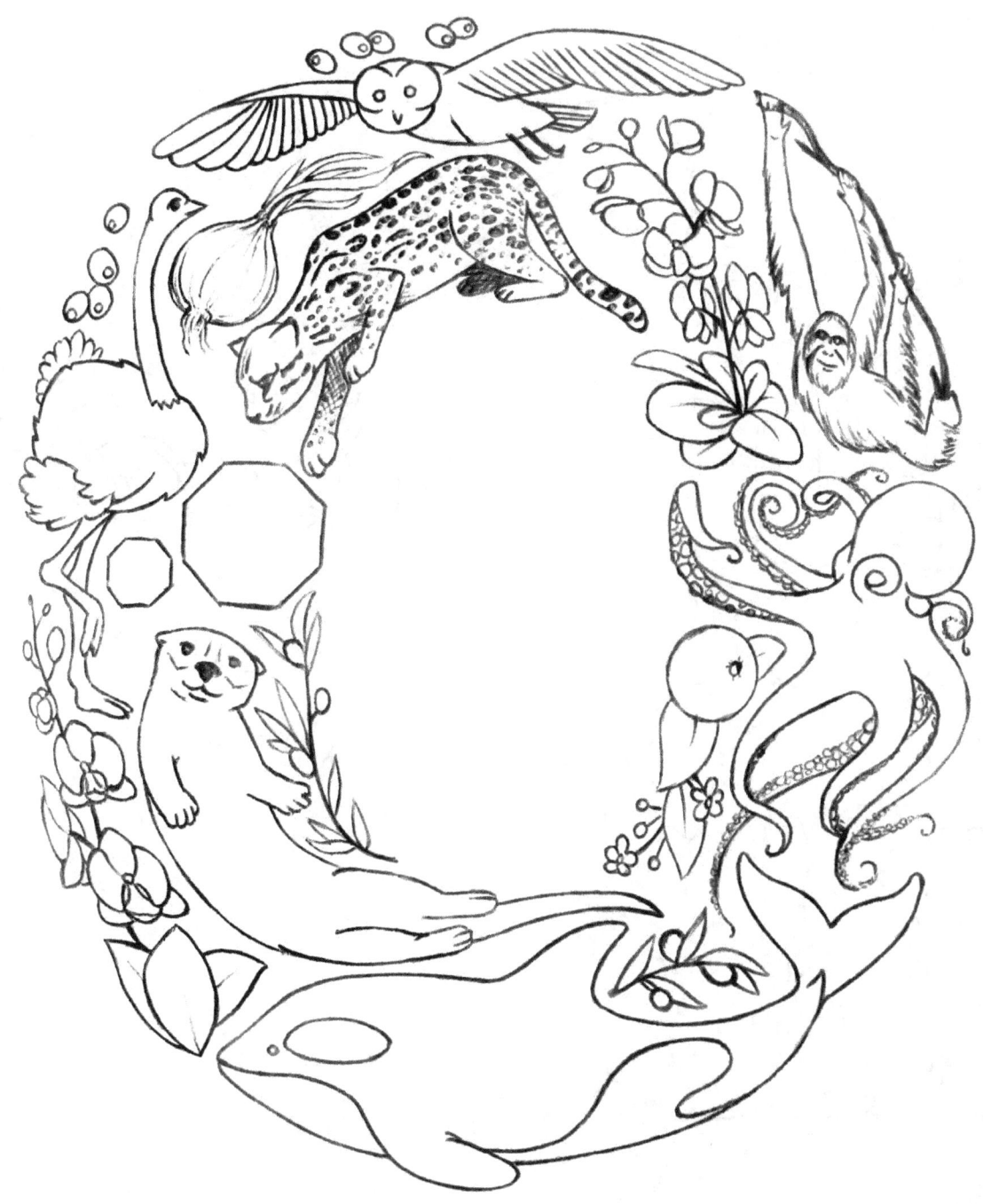

Can you find...

Ocelot, Octagon, Octopus, Olives, Onions, Orca, Orange, Orangutan, Orchid, Ostrich, Otter, Owl

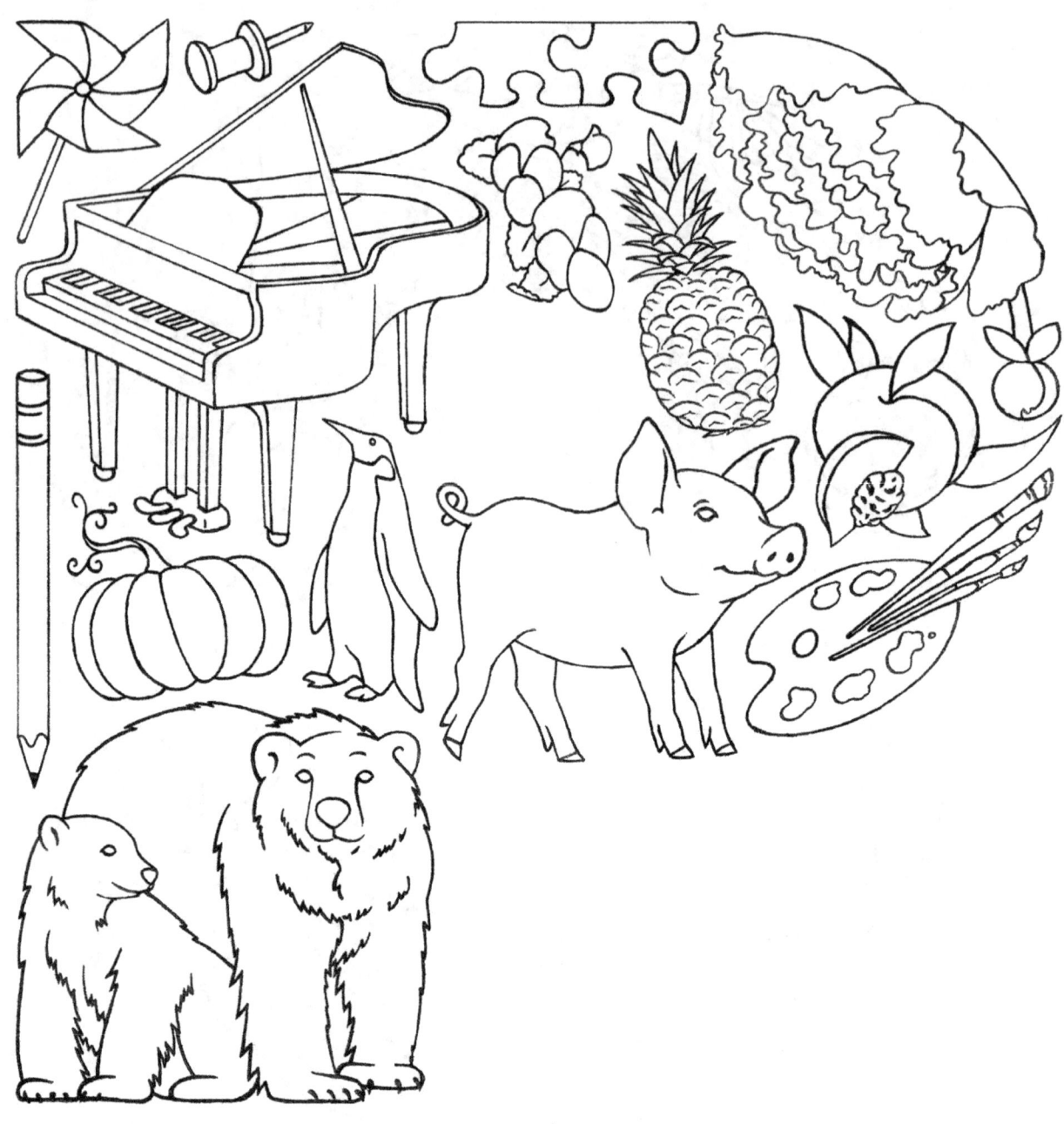

Do you see these objects?

Paint Palette, Pansy, Peach, Pencil, Penguin, Peony, Piano, Pig, Pineapple, Pinwheel, Polar Bear, Pumpkin, Pushpin, Puzzle

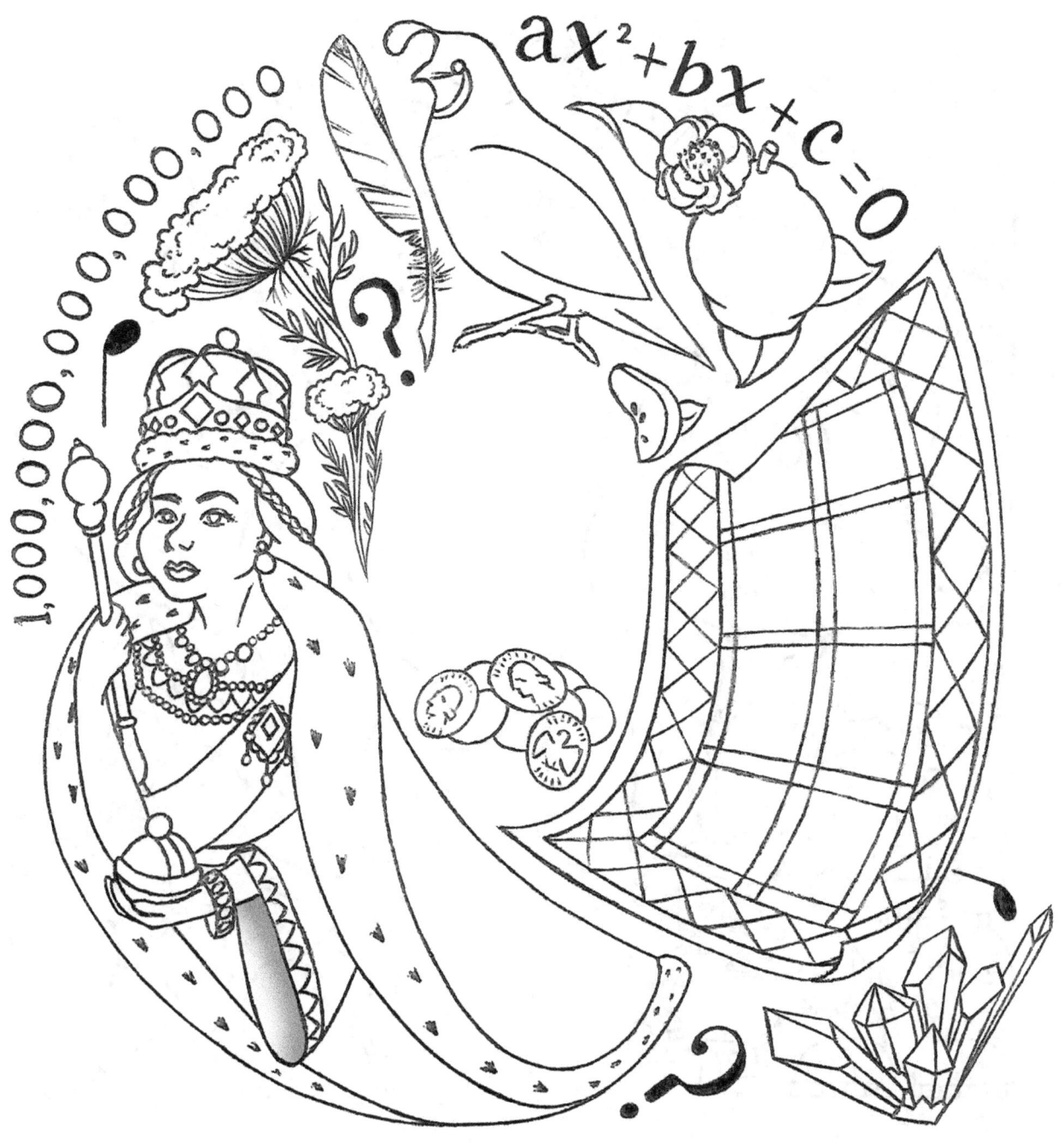

Can you find these things?

Quadratic Equation, Quadrillion, Quail, Quarters, Quarter Note, Quartz, Queen, Queen Anne's Lace, Question Mark, Quill, Quilt, Quince

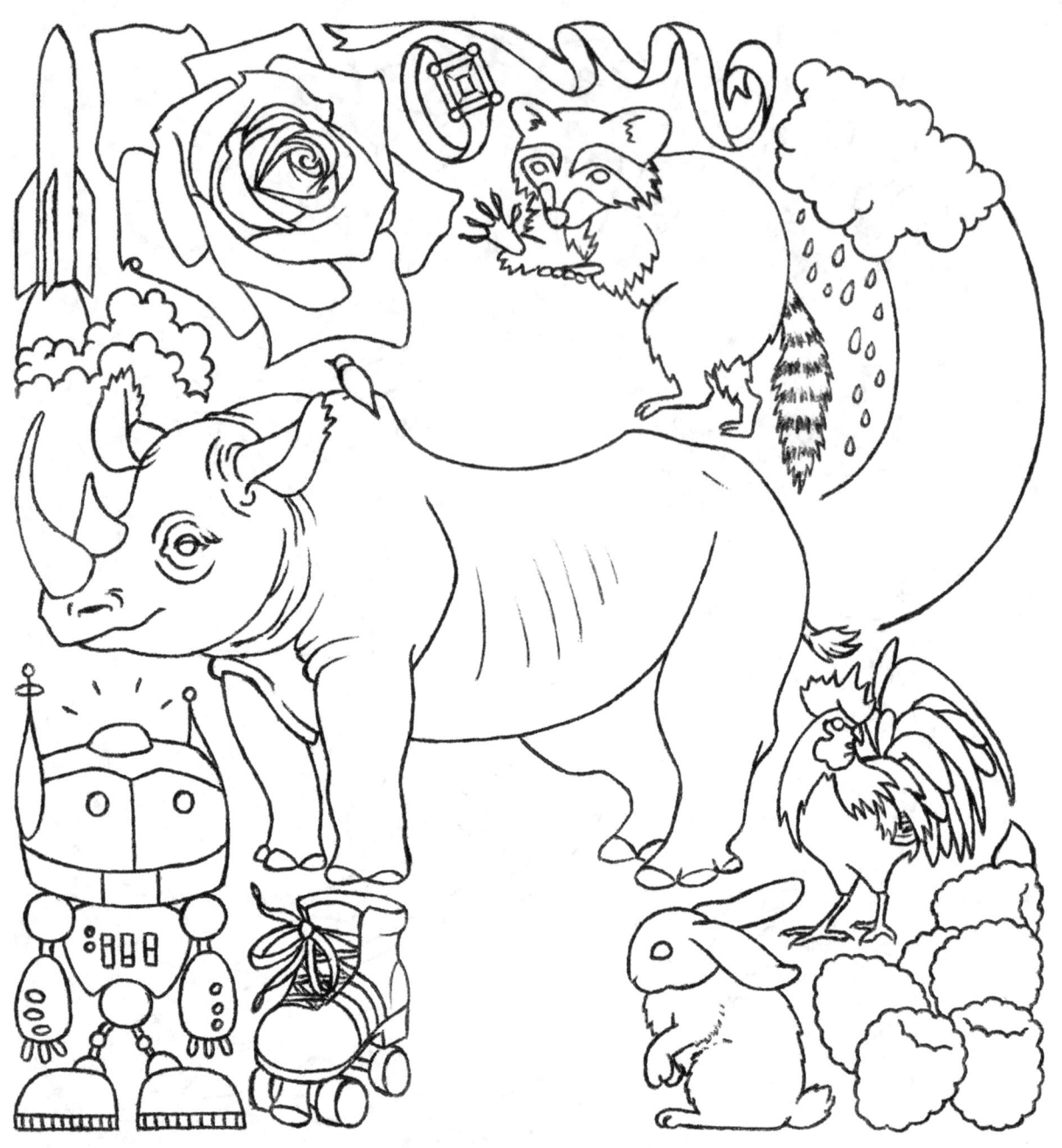

Look for...

Rabbit, Raccoon, Rain, Rainbow, Raincloud, Raspberries, Rhinoceros, Ribbon, Robot, Rocket, Roller Skate, Rose, Rooster, Ruby Ring

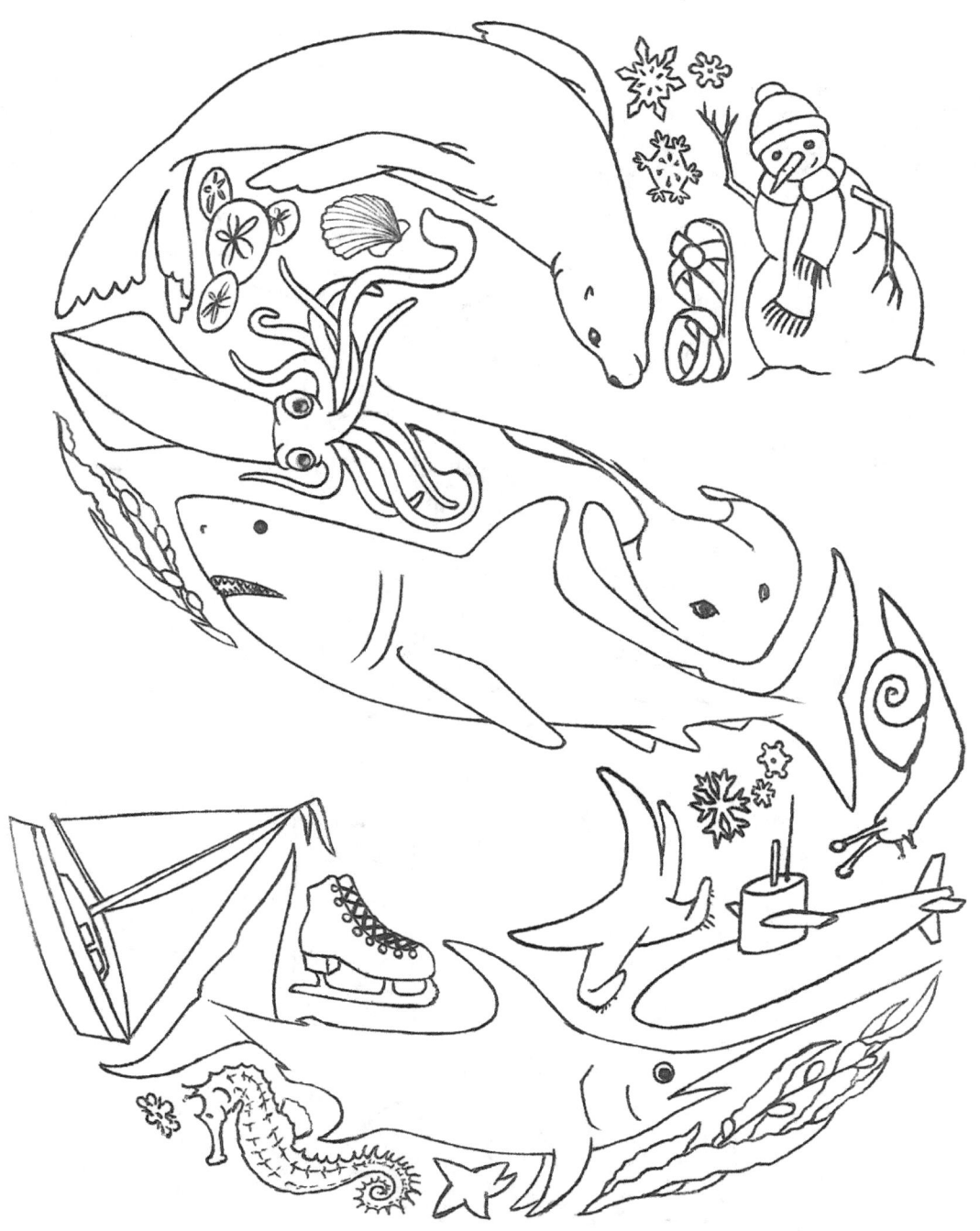

Can you find these objects?

Sailboat, Sandal, Sand Dollar, Scallop Shell, Sea Lion, Seahorse, Seastar, Seaweed, Shark, Skate, Snail, Snowflakes, Snowman, Squid, Stingray, Submarine, Swordfish

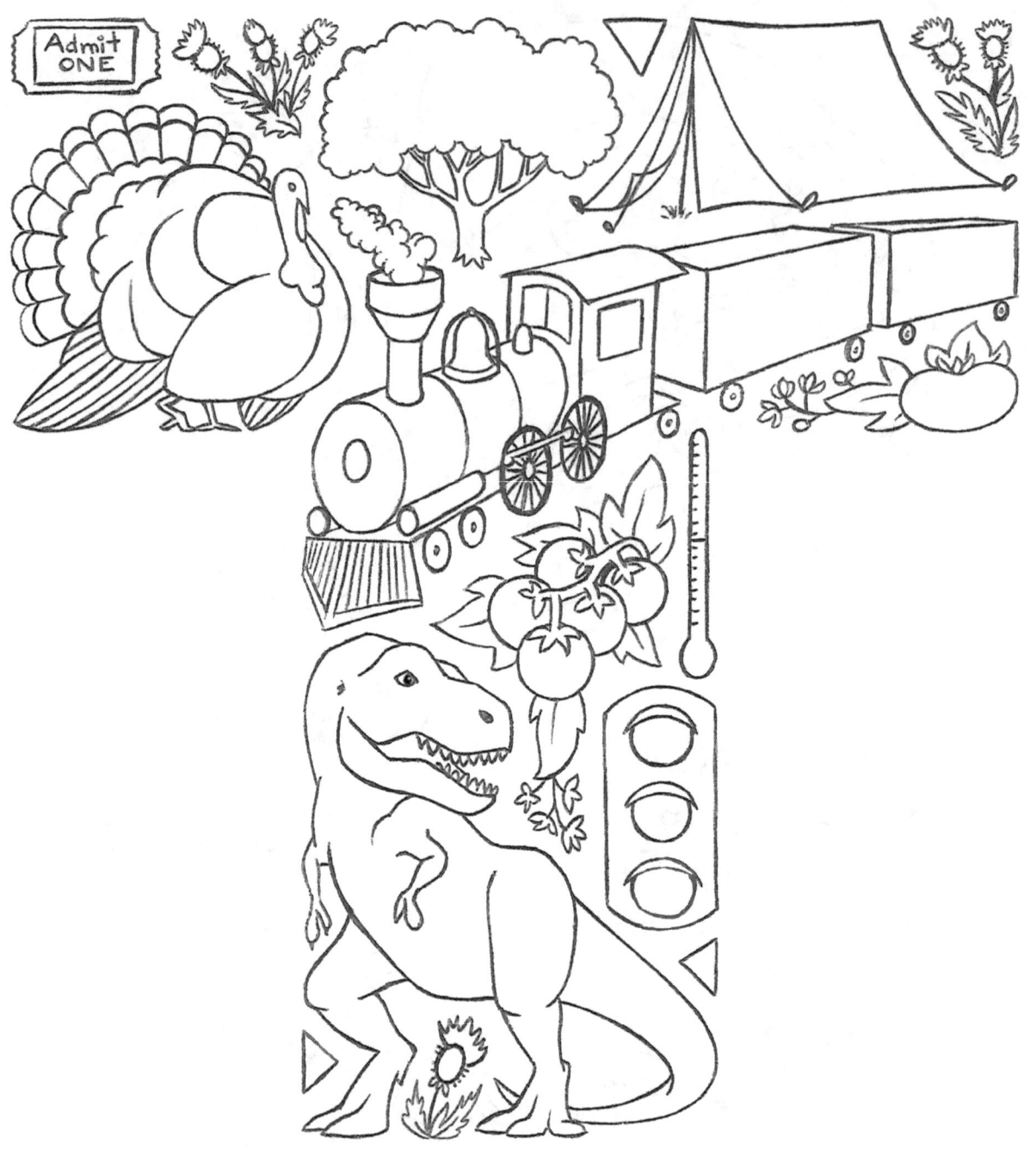

Look for these things.

Tent, Thermometer, Thistle, Ticket, Tomato, Traffic Light, Train, Tree, Triangle, Turkey, Tyrannosaurus Rex

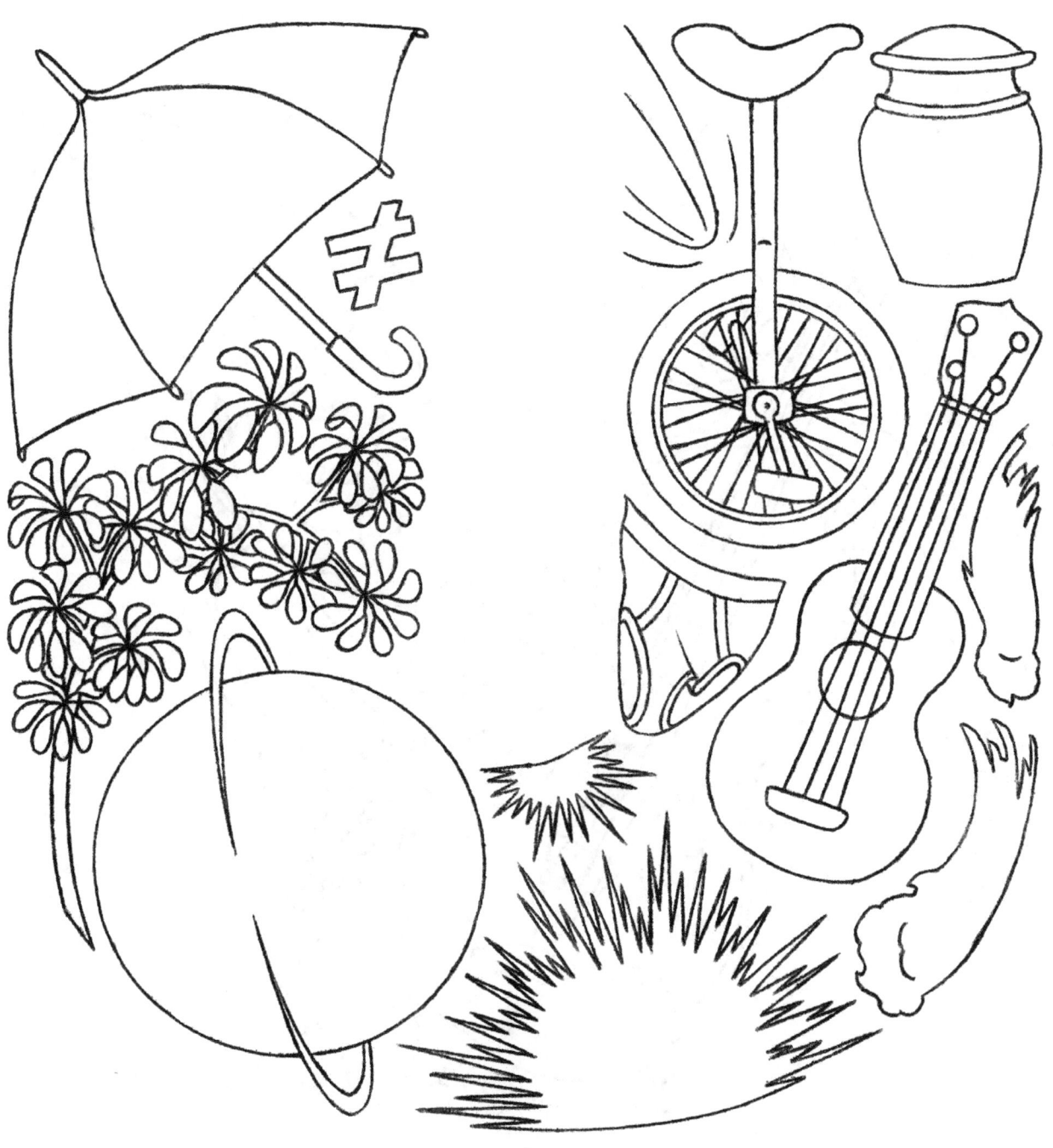

Do you see...

Ukulele, Umbrella, Umbrella Plant, Ultramarine, Ultra-Violet, Umber, Underwear, Unequal, Unicycle, Uranus, Urchin, Urn

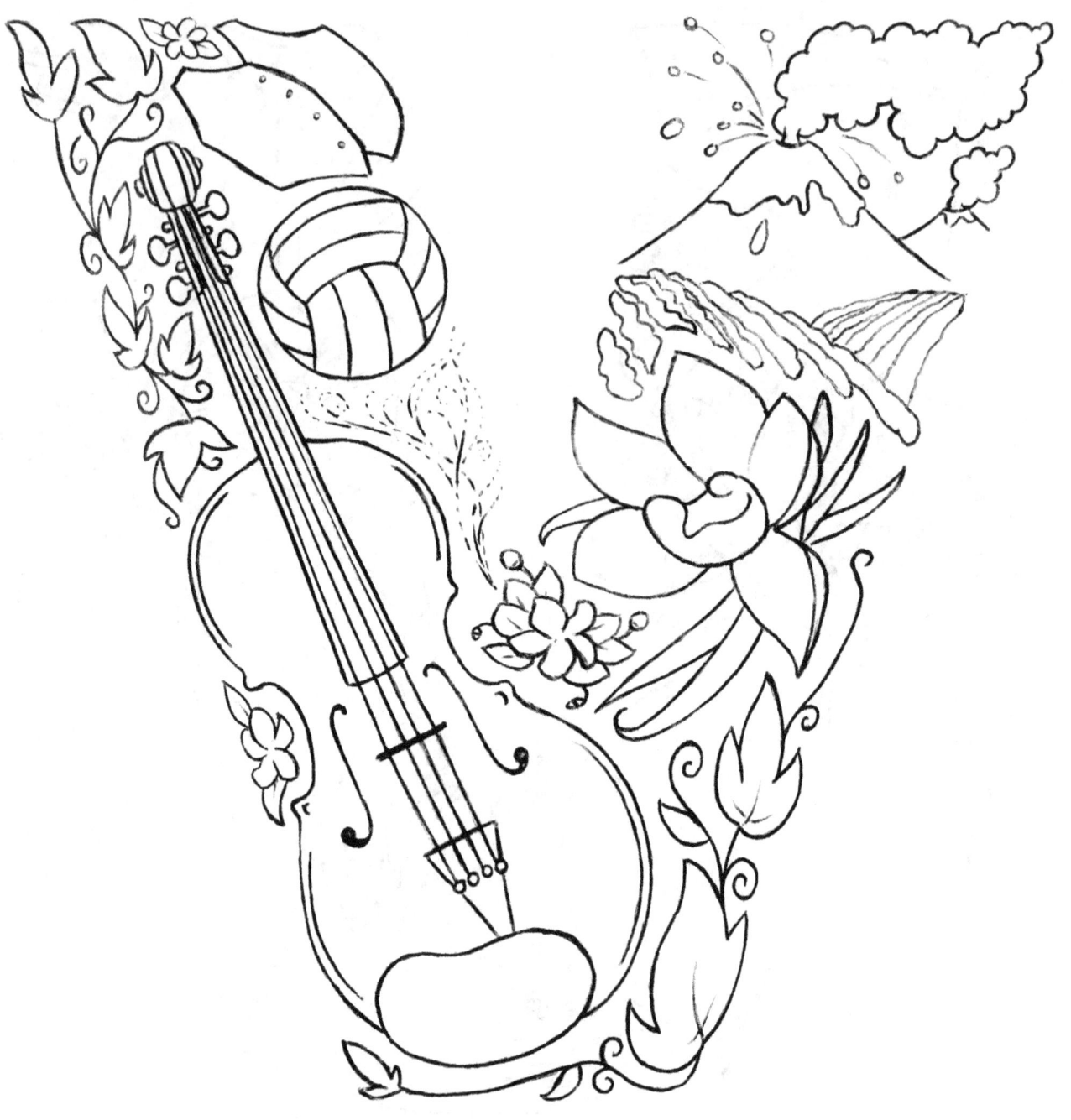

Look for these objects.

Vanilla Bean and Vanilla Flower, Vapor, Vest, Vine, Vineyard, Violet, Violin, Volcano, Volleyball

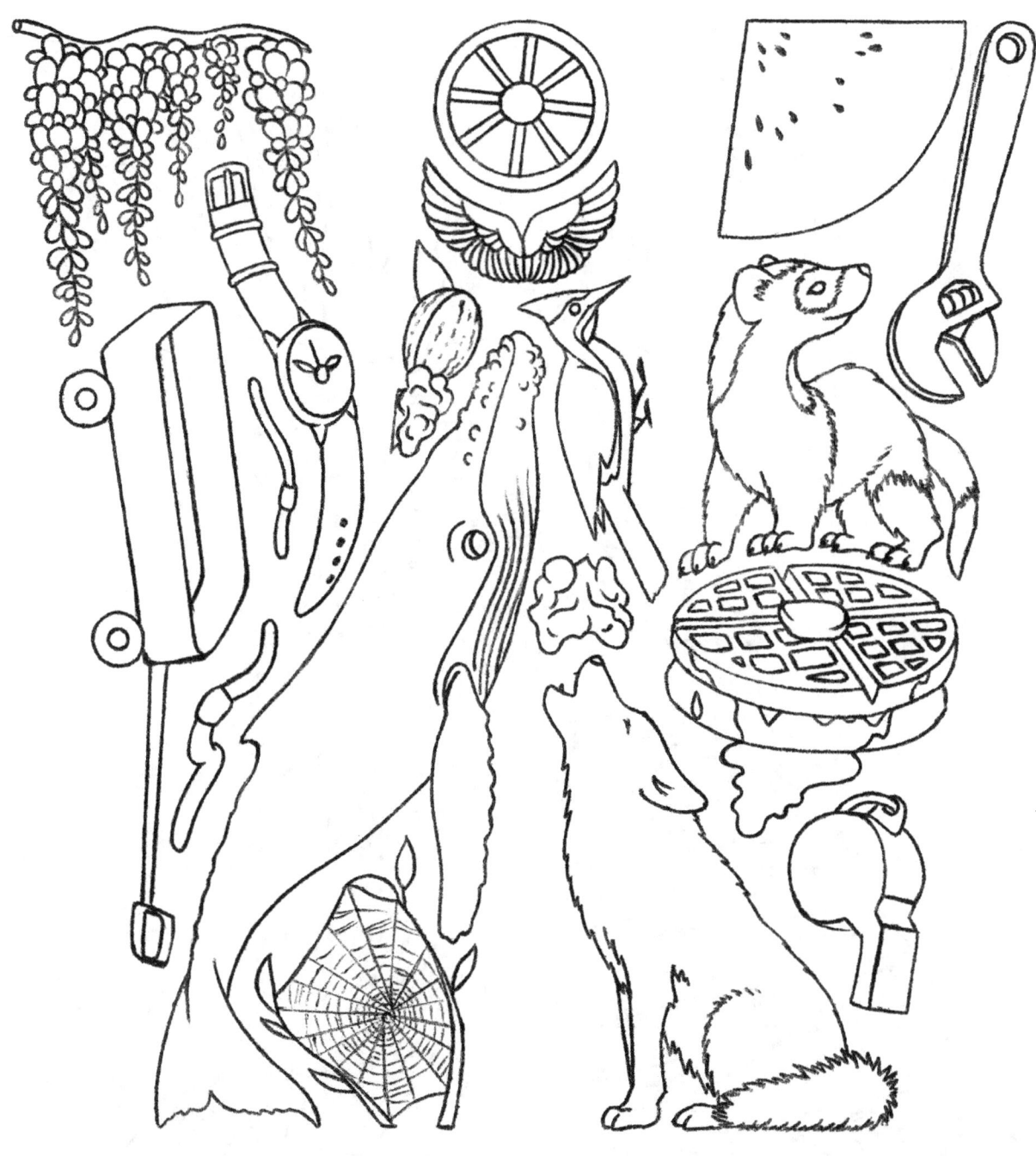

Do you see these things?

Wagon, Waffle, Walnuts, Watch, Watermelon, Weasel, Web, Whale, Wheel, Whistle, Wings, Wisteria, Wolf, Woodpecker, Worm, Wrench

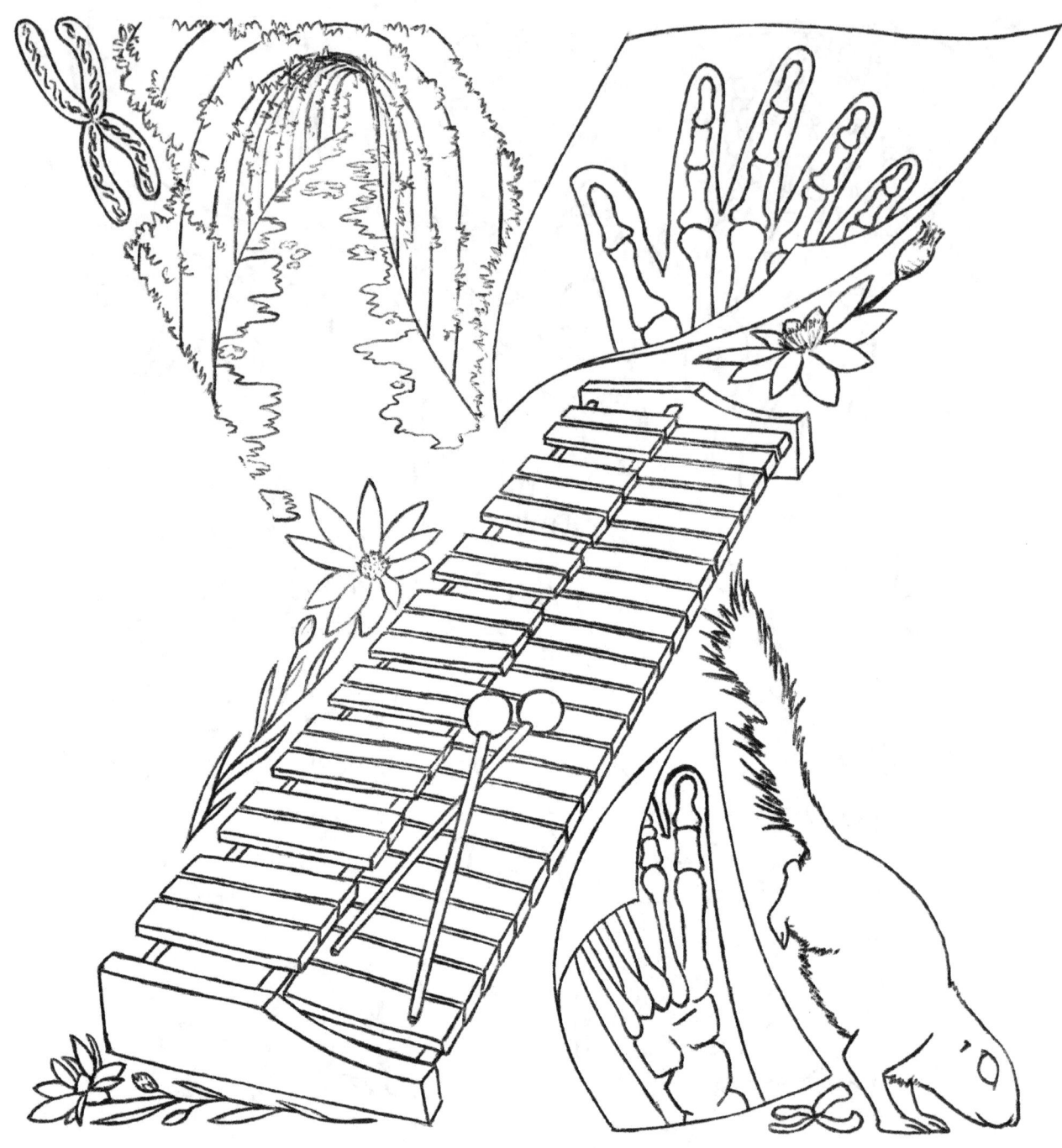

Can you find...

X-Chromosome, Xeranthemum Flower, Xerus (African Squirrel), Xylophone, Xyst (Arched Garden Path)

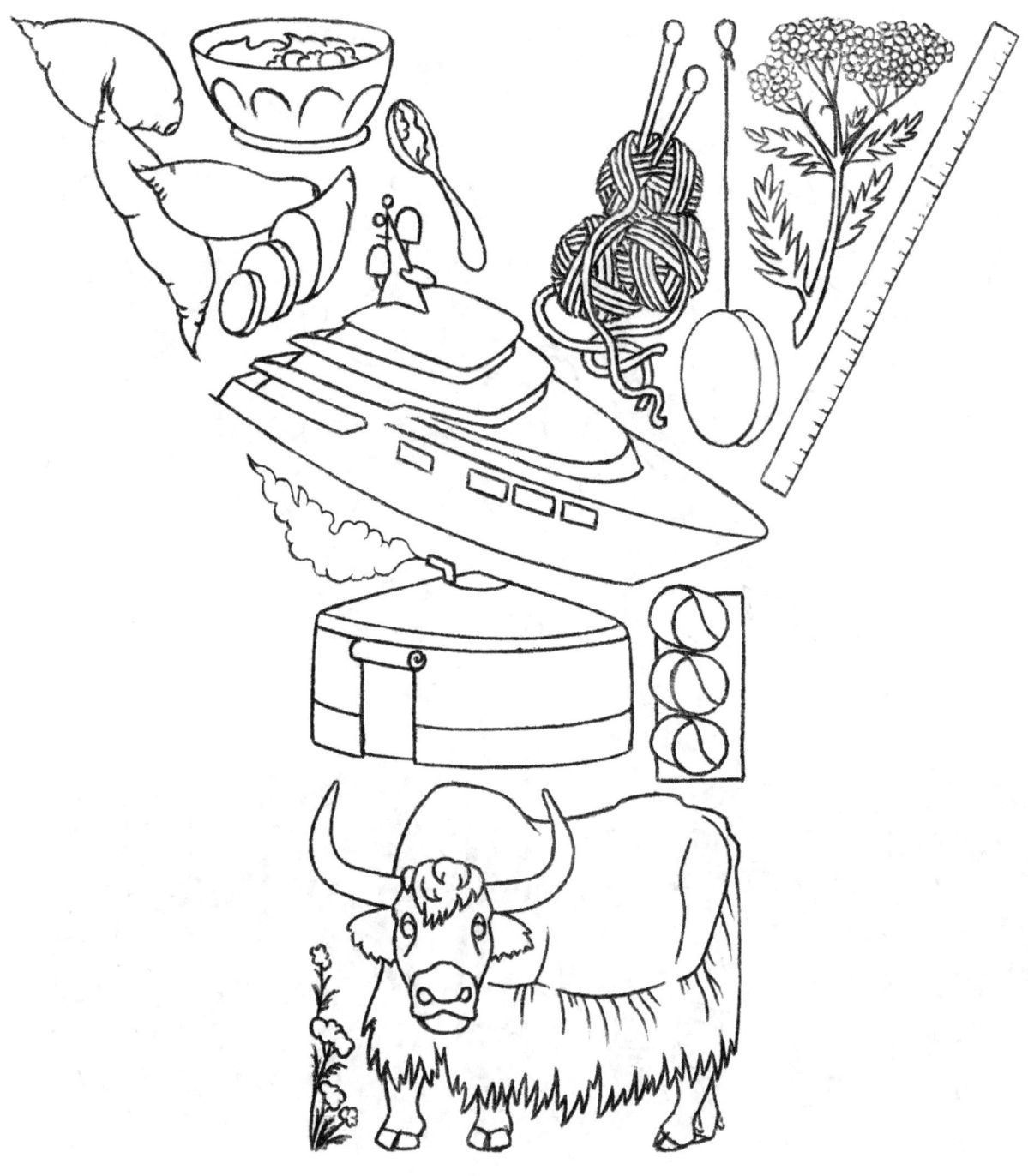

Do you see these objects?

Yacht, Yak, Yardstick, Yarn, Yarrow, Yams, Yellow Light, Yo-yo, Yogurt, Yurt

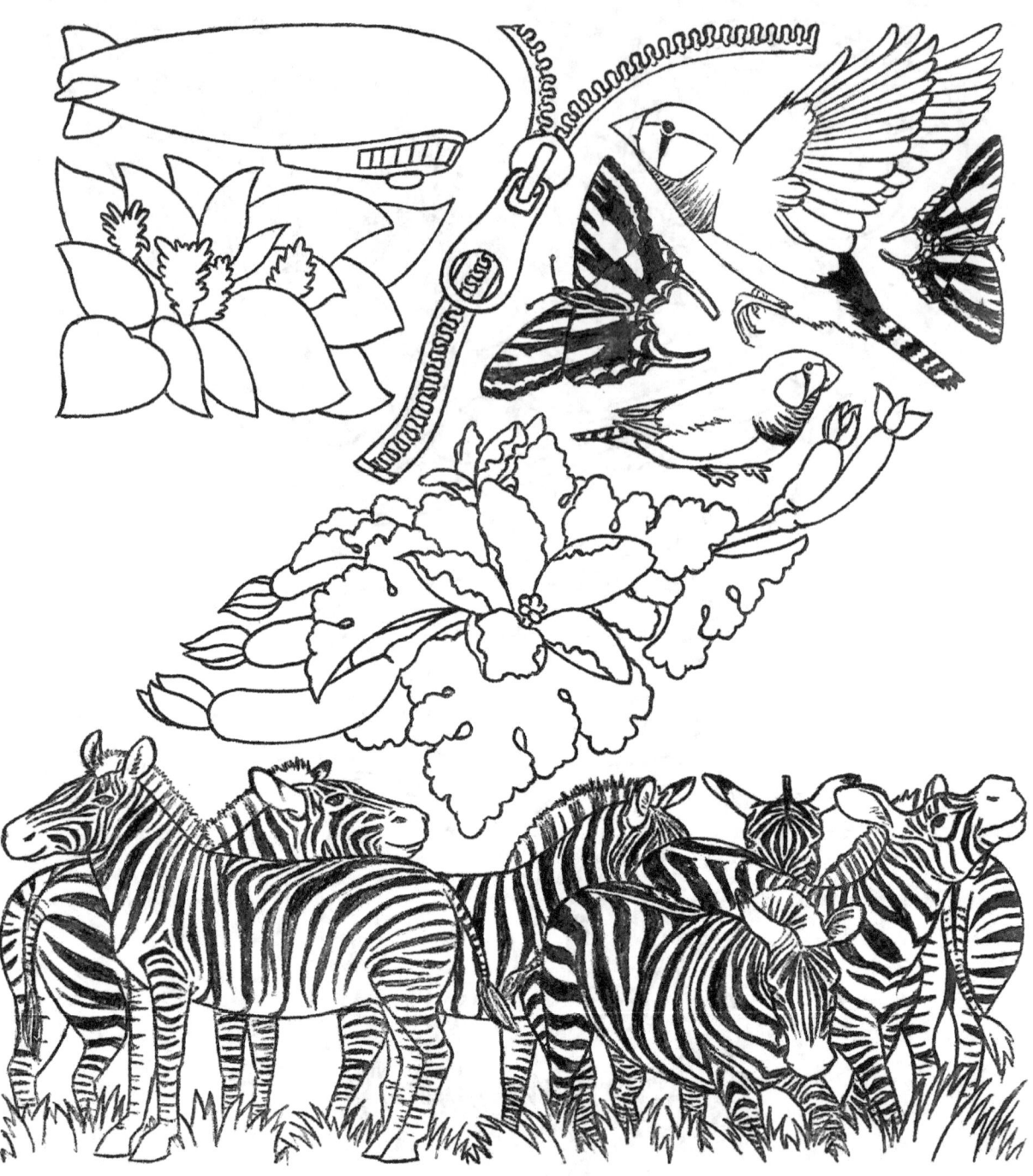

Can you find these things?

Zebra, Zebra Finch, Zebra Plant, Zebra Swallowtail Butterfly, Zeppelin, Zipper, Zucchini

www.ingramcontent.com/pod-product-compliance
Lightning Source LLC
Chambersburg PA
CBHW081148170526
45158CB00009BA/2768